# THE LAST PROPHET

By

J. Climenstein

# Introduction

I am sharing with you a life changing event and experience that,with much inner searching and the assistance of those around me, I am now attempting to put you in the driver's seat of my life during that time. This story is based on experiences that took place between the dates of Wednesday, July 23$^{rd}$ through Friday, July 25$^{th}$, 2014, in the northwest state of Washington in the USA. These three days and the days preceding this event are what some would call an "awakening" of sorts. I will account to you the best I can of what happened. This event, at times, has left me broken, as "what is seen cannot be unseen."

## Day One

It was summer time in the green state of Washington and an overcast sky insulated the summer heat. I find myself in the basement of my home, in my "man cave," where I had been finding myself for the past three months.

I had gotten notice that my unemployment benefits would end at the end of the month. After leaving a lengthy career in the United States military, I found my hope dwindling as job applications and interviews, one after the other netted no results for me, except frustration and now, serious depression. It wasn't due to the lack of trying. I applied night and day, interviewed often, yet still was not able to make it through an interview without "war" related questions being asked; at least that was my perception. They'd ask and I'd tell them. As soon as I would, I could see their demeanor change. My military experience was geared towards the training and carrying out war on the enemy. It was my military job and now I realize that I just might intimidate the regular civilian conducting interviews.

I am a war veteran and served just shy of fifteen years. The climb in the ranks had been quick as it was the height of the wars in Iraq and Afghanistan. I had been deployed to Afghanistan as a Platoon Sergeant. It was not in a glamorous job while in the military, but I did my share of "bringing it" to the enemy during a tour to Afghanistan in Kunar Province during 2011-2012. When I returned home, the ongoing process and adjustment to civilian life was just not happening and I hated myself for not being able to make the transition back with more expedience and clarity. I had been diagnosed with PTSD while in the service following the deployment to Afghanistan and had lost my military medical insurance a few months prior, so I was not in any sort of treatment. The depression hit me kind of hard.

Now, and for the previous days leading up to this day, the bouts of memories begin to set in again and were coming at me strong. Like I said, "what is seen cannot be unseen." I'd try to fight them off, yet they'd come back even with more intensity and clarity. As these memories that were playing like a re-run movie reel in my head; the decisions I made that affected the lives of others and then in retrospect, calling them "stupid decisions," were taking me down, one at a time. I really hated myself at this point.

So, this is where I find myself, reflecting

and battling this horrid depression. Then I hear the mail truck pass by my house from the basement. As I retrieve the mail, I see that a letter from my life insurance that had carried over from the military is amongst the now many bills that are piling up. The letter states that unless I bring my premiums current, my coverage will be terminated at the end of the month. Great! No money, no job, no prospects, and now my life insurance is getting cut. How much more could I let down my family? That's when the thoughts came flooding in as to a way out. The pressure is hitting me. I start reflecting on the man I once was to whom I've become. I reflect on my family and how useless I now see myself to them. My wife, my beautiful wife, was a full-time student now, thanks to the military GI bill that I was able to transfer to her, as I had gotten my master's degree while still actively serving. Along with the monthly stipend and the unemployment benefits, there was barely enough money to cover the bills, not even taking into consideration any extras or emergencies. The credit cards were being maxed out and with no hope of finding a job at all, I was losing hope. Questions and phrases like, "Am I really worthless?" began flooding my mind and then and might I say, with very much clarity.

# The Moment

I was very aware and well-informed of the number of veterans committing suicide a day, twenty-two, in fact across the country. I now found myself contemplating getting it over with. I was home alone in my man cave, my own space, and I began to premeditate how I would carry this out. I started thinking back on my military service and started pulling from it the very experience that would overlay what I was now planning to do. I was familiar with how the military treated wives of veterans in this situation as I was one of the very officers who assisted during one of these instances. I was a Casualty Assistance Officer and once helped a young widow who had lost her husband due to non-military action. He had died by having a standoff with the El Paso, Texas police where he ultimately shot himself in the chest, dying on the scene. I was not given the full story; however, I remember giving her a check for $100,000 the day after he had killed himself. It was that quick. A few weeks later, I drove her to a bank to deposit yet another $400,000 from his life insurance pay out. I even remember thinking at that time, "us soldiers are worth more dead than alive" and it stuck with me. My life insurance was due to expire at the end of the month and knowing that it would pay out even in the event of suicide, the thought of doing it began looking better and better. I then went upstairs to my gun safe and pulled out my AR-15 and a loaded magazine. I kept my guns near where I slept and always kept a loaded magazine at the ready. I know, sounds a little institutionalized, granted, it was where I was in the moment. So, I took the rifle down to my man cave and I began to stare into the dark open space. There are windows that allow some light from windows to the area, other than that, the man cave is reflecting the dreary from the outside. I just stood there and stared out one of the windows to the clouds in the sky. I begin the process of how to carry this out once again in my mind and this time with *real* emphasis as the barrel of the gun is pointed at my head. My head begins to fill with the thoughts like:

"You can do this for your family!"

"What good am I to them now?"

I must make you aware that as an atheist at this time. I saw nothing morally wrong with what I was planning to do. I feared no repercussions from any outside force with this strong atheistic belief. In my mind, I had convinced myself that committing suicide would help my family more than me sticking around and being unable to provide for them.

# The Awakening

I sat there motionless in the dreary dark basement, full of self-pity, with the rifle's barrel still pointed at my head and something happened. I asked once, "Why me?"

And then a second time in a louder voice, "*Why me?*"

And then a *third* time, **"God, why me?"**

All of the sudden I felt a lightning bolt of energy hit my entire body. My finger let go of the trigger on the rifle and as if I were watching a movie of my life in my mind's eye, my life began flashing before my eyes. I couldn't see anything besides this movie playing in my head and at the same time began feeling a kind of warmth in my body that started in my mid-section and extended up my spine to my head; a tingling sensation pulsated across my body. The movie started in my childhood and showed me every time that I had perceived myself as being the victim. I got to see through the eyes of my adversaries as the visions seemed to communicate with me. They were showing me how in every action that I had been the victim had been perceived incorrectly. It was playing out that perceiving you are a victim is only due to your intimate perception. Situation after situation, I could see that all the times I had been done wrong, had just been perceived that way by the older version of me. The big picture began to dawn on me. Perception is a casualty to actions and every action witnessed has a preceptory influence on the observer. It all started to make sense. All of it. It was not that I was a bad human being or that I had done something wrong, all of it was designed to be the way in which it played out. *We are all connected!*

A smile filled my face. I came out of my depression into an understanding of what had transpired. I was confused yet accepting. I was still staring out one of the windows in my basement at the overcast sky, now filled with puffy white clouds. As my vision focused better and narrowed, I could see a light off in the distance, a brilliant white light that just hovered there just below the clouds. I had been staring at the light for the entire time, yet had not noticed it before. Then without much fanfare, the light drifted back into the clouds and that was the start of what would be the craziest set of days I have ever been through in my life. I don't have the answers to what happened, yet my hope is that somebody out there who reads this book will understand and be able to make sense of it all, at least part of it or any of it at this point, would be nice. Has God intervened and if so, why? What was God? What was the light I had witnessed through the window in that very moment of deep and sincere sorrow and pain, yet with specific clarity? These questions would be attempted to be answered in the following days as I continued to gain a new filter in this life. In other words, this was indeed a whole new perspective and outlook on life that I had never taken up to this point. Remember, I am an atheist still, at this point in time. When I say filter, I mean a way of looking at things or perception, one that is gained by experience. Everybody has a unique set of filters on how they look at life and their reality. One could so far as to say that your filter is like coding in a computer that allows it to display a webpage.

The webpage in this instance would be the perception that your unique filter allows you to gaze upon.

The rest of that day I felt connected to something. The tingling sensations did not stop after the experience, continuing and keeping me in this state of mind, intensifying the effect that allowed me to know that something indeed was still happening and ongoing. Whatever it was, it was still there in my awareness. My head would tingle whenever I would have a new thought that led into a new concept for me. The feeling was one that I can only describe, as a gamer, as a type of "leveling up" or at least, that's all I was going to call it in this moment. I know that probably does not make sense, yet that's exactly how I felt. It felt like I was connected to the knowledge bank of all of humanity during this period. I could pull from it like pulling out a DVD player and picking a favorite DVD to watch. I found myself asking questions out loud and instantly I would close my eyes and see an answer to those questions represented by shapes, colors, and sometimes full movies playing out in my mind like a set of Lego blocks. During this time, which I am now calling an "awakening," my body and mind were alive with all the things I felt. The next couple of days would show me more, as this is only the

## Day Two

I awoke to a sensational urge to write. I began the day early as my need for sleep had dissipated. I felt refreshed after waking up and spent time with my wife, telling her how much I loved her. I spent time with my children and grand-children. As I looked out the window, I could see that a family of deer was directly outside of my house. As I opened the door and went outside, I could feel them. This is where is begins to sound crazy; I felt that I could communicate with them and even went as far as to walk up on one of the males and in this moment and not to my surprise, it did not get aggressive. I stood within five feet of the larger one out of the herd and it just stared back at me. I showed no intentions; the proud male deer seemed to connect to the understanding. You see, just as we have filters to ourselves and our intimate surroundings, animals have much the same filters. Their experience in the moment dictates how they react to other animals. I could feel that it was not scared. It was proud and the same time, clear that it wanted me to acknowledge that by keeping my distance. I obliged, kind of gave a nod, went back into the house and straight down to the man cave, where I began writing with great and specific intensity and specificity. A flood of information came pouring from my mind as I began asking questions that were answered in quick succession. It felt that I was on auto-pilot that day. I could not pull myself away from my laptop for even a few minutes without finding myself back there writing. All sorts of innovative ideas began to emerge. I wrote from societal problems to the existence of God as I navigated a narrative with whatever it was that I was communicating with. There was an invisible connection during these days that I cannot fully comprehend. I have plenty of guesses to what it could have been, however, to this day have been unable to identify it, without a doubt. I'd like to think of this connection as sort of like what we experience whenever we use Wi-Fi. We cannot see the connection, yet we can tell if our electronic device is connected, nonetheless. At the same time, I thought that my mind was coming up with these great ideas, however, what transpired and continued to happen the following days tells me differently.

# The Numbers

A remarkable happening occurred following the initial experience. I began seeing consecutive numbers such as 1111 or 333 all over the place. From clocks to the change given at a local store; this affliction still plagues me to this day. I've tried to share this phenomenon with some, yet most dismiss it and say that numbers have no meaning. To these ones, I understand the concept of seeing things that are outside of the norm are contrary to what their filter allows them to understand. Only those who are afflicted with this condition know what I mean when I say, there is a type of undeniable intelligence to the random occurrences of the numbers manifesting themselves. It is not randomness that brings them into existence, it is quite the opposite. Some say the numbers are angelic and come from the heavens and that they mark those meant to be saved. I'm still not clear to the truth on this; however, I'm beginning to believe that there may be some validity to this claim. That explanation is not relevant to the story at hand so I will save the explanation for a future writing, as my intimate filter has allowed me to see the outside world differently than anyone else. I understand, that in reality our filters allow us to see the world through our own set of eyes, utilizing our own filters, in which in turn translates to the subjective reality we all live within.

One could argue that the objective reality is where we reside, yet, I would point out that as understanding and knowledge are increased, our perceived objective reality is also prone to changing. This happens more often than realized.

When new discoveries are made or we have an understanding of a concept at a new level, our "world view" changes. It's inevitable. As we increase in understanding, the objective reality is better defined and honed to our experiential understanding. Truly, until you step back and get out of your own way, your own ego, your own filter, one cannot see objective reality as our own perspective as perceived reality gets in the way. Only a small percentage of people who live on this planet have a true grasp on objective reality and the entire picture as to how this works. It is because of how our opinions and/or feelings rather than facts or evidence, that are tossed around and how these somewhat knee-jerk responses consistently get in the way of many seeing thus said objective reality. In other words, our subjectiveness gets in the way of us seeing it.

You think you know it, right? Well, it was once thought that the earth was flat! Then science came along and proved it was a sphere. Both scenarios were taken as the objective reality of their day, yet only one is known to be the true objective reality of today. Will it be the objective reality of tomorrow? Time will tell and as we increase in our knowledge base, so too does our viewpoint on what is objective versus what is subjective. By the way, objective reality is open to the interpretation by the observer, yes? Can't the observer be wrong in their interpretation just as well as it is now being interpreted from their subjective reality? These are the types of questions I asked myself on the second day of my experience and frantically, like a scribe, I wrote down every tidbit. Finally, I went to bed around one o'clock in the morning. At this point my body didn't require too much sleep;

I got in a few hours. I knew that as soon as I woke up, I would be fresh and ready to tackle a new pursuit. I had passion in my mind as something big was about to happen, I just didn't know what. I was at peace and the excitement was getting to me.

## Day Three

I woke up earlier than usual, having only slept for a few hours the night before. I got up, had some coffee and around 9:00 AM, I went into my bedroom to wake up my wife. Just before I woke her up, I'd been thinking about a camping trip to just get out to nature and away from all the details of life. I got the urge to camp with my family and here is where the previous days leading up to this day began to merge. As soon as I woke her up, she told me about a dream she had just before I woke her up. She said, "I had a dream that we went camping and there was a forest and a river right beside our campsite."

Shocked, yet not surprised at all, I internalize what just happened. I didn't say anything to her, yet wondered how my mind connected with her mind on the same thought level that I was having. How did the same thoughts as I was having enter her thoughts, seemingly, in dream state of exactly what I was thinking about before I had woke her up? Again, I took this as a sign.

# The Signs

One after another, the signs are coming in different shapes and forms. Everything from the combination of numbers such as the 1111 discussed earlier, to the thoughts one holds at the time of something coming into your gaze that fits with that thought. Really, I only understood them for what they were, as at this point, I am definitely an observer of what is happening around me. Synchronicities filled my collective consciousness at the time. Her talking about camping directly after I had a thought about camping was the beginning of the merge. She was part of showing me the path, as if it was laid out in front of me. It was my path, yet now she is with me and is definitely along for the ride, quite consciously, I might add. I have come to believe that all of us are on a path in this life. It is the road that presents itself at any given time and no matter how you perceive that road in front of you; the path is the one with the least resistance. Instinctively, I said,

"Let's go camping!"

That's all it took to seal the deal. We were off for the day with my son and my oldest grandson. Understand this; I did not camp on my off time while I served in the military. I had my share of "camping" during my time in the service and did not look at camping as some sort of thing to do recreationally on my off time. We had no camping gear so our first stop was at the local Walmart to pick up the necessary supplies. Really, we had no plan. We had no way of knowing even where to go camping, just a slight knowledge that Mount Rainier National Forest had a couple of campgrounds. So, we loaded up our vehicle with all the brand new equipment and that is the direction we headed.

# The Path

I had an inner feeling that I was going camping to meet something; yet I had no idea of what that would be. I would just be alert to it. I had the overwhelming sensation that whatever I was looking for would be found on that camping trip. I reserved myself around my son and wife, not letting onto them that anything out of the ordinary was happening with me. I internalized these feelings; I didn't want them to think I had lost my mind fully and really, at this time, quite frankly, I wasn't questioning my mind, I just didn't know what to expect going forward. It was this interaction; this connection; and how was it happening. This is what I was questioning? How is my wife involved in my mind?! I mean, we love each other; however, never have we ever experienced anything like this before between us. And it's still coming at us; we just are here experiencing something as one unit and my son too! How cool is that? I'm at least, so thankful for that! The trip started out with us traveling down the highway into the Mount Rainier National Park. We stopped off at the last sign of civilization in Ashford, Washington before entering the park and we sat there eating gas station sandwiches. As I was alert to my surroundings, I noticed a vehicle that had been behind us the entire time and now was parked beside us. I thought to myself whether or not they were on the same journey and then dismissed it. We finished our sandwiches and I noticed a Park Ranger was there. I asked him where the campgrounds were located and he directed me to drive up the road about two to three miles and the first set of campsites would be off to the left. I thanked him and we were back on

our way heading into the park.

# The Big Campsite

After travelling further down Paradise Road E, we arrived around noon and were excited to pick out our campsite. I was confident we had everything we needed to make a good camping trip and that finally we could begin this adventure. There was no river directly next to the campsites, yet it was definitely within walking distance. The Nisqually River was across the main road from the campsites. The head shed was just inside the entrance where we stopped. There was a kiosk where you could purchase a campsite. I paid for a campsite and received a receipt from the machine. I read the instructions and in order to reserve a site you were to drive around until you found an open site and then clip your receipt to the sign at the front of the campsite that everyone had at their entrance and in plain view.

"Now our adventure is really beginning," I thought to myself.

As we headed even deeper into the forest, the campsites were sectioned off alphabetically, so starting with the letter "A" section of the site; we began our way around through the letters. We had been circling around for almost an hour and still were unable to find a single open campsite. All of them had a "reserved" receipt clipped to the sign at their entrance. We finally found an open site. I slow down to the post where there is no reserved ticket on it to ask my wife,

"Does this look good?"

She looked out the passenger window to confirm that it was free of the receipt and said, "Yes, this will work."

We pulled our vehicle into the space and then something happened. A thought came over my mind that told me to look at the sign again. So I stopped what I was doing and said, "Let me check the sign again."

There was no one around and most of the sites that we had driven by for the past hour had only the receipt attached to their signs. They had been void of any obvious activity to even make us believe that anyone had been there. No cars, no people, just receipts indicating that the site was and had been "reserved." I walked over to the post where the sign was to the edge of the campsite where I found a receipt attached to it *and* it wasn't ours! I looked at my wife and asked, "Are you sure there was no receipt on this sign out here?"

She answered, "Yes. Why? Is there one there now?"

Perplexed to say the least, we both shook our heads collectively. Almost in silence, we gathered up what little bit we had gotten out of the car, got back into the car and were just going to cut our losses at this point and go back home. We were a bit frustrated, yet it had been a beautiful ride and we had plenty of time to get back home before it got totally dark. With a strange feeling about me, I began driving out to the front of the park. We had given up our hope of camping by now and just agreed to take the fee as a loss instead of trying to get a refund, let alone, find another campground within the park. Just as I am about to exit the park, I kind of sighed while having a feeling of empowerment at the same time and said to my wife, "Well, we tried."

Just as she is agreeing and our hopes of camping is kind of crushed, I see a park ranger off to the side of the road walking alone. I stopped and rolled down my window to address him. "Sir, do you know if any of the campsites are open currently or, where we might find one?"

He kind of chuckled and said that all the sites had been fully booked and that I wouldn't find anything else in the park for the weekend. I then asked him, "Okay, so can you tell me where to go to get a refund for the site I just purchased?"

He told me to go to the entrance to the park, go up to the head shed and there I could get a full refund. I take his advice and direction and on the way out of the campsite, I stop at the head shed. I tell my wife that I'll be right back and proceed to walk up to the shed. There is another park ranger inside and I begin the explanation of why I want a refund.

"Sir, I just paid for a campsite and found out by another ranger that the campground is fully booked. May I get a refund?"

He starts the process of giving me a refund and being the friendly me, I started talking to him. I told him that we had our hearts set on camping and it had been a little disappointing that all the sites were already booked. He apologized for the inconvenience and ends the conversation as the business at hand had been concluded. Just as I started to walk away, he said, "Wait, there are a few free campsites that are primitive in nature without any kind of services," he said in a distinct directive voice.

Intrigued, I turned back around and he shows me a map where the campsites are located. Without asking for exact directions, as I have a good understanding of how maps work, I see the quickest route from where I am to where I now needed to go to get to the campsite. It was located outside of the park along the Nisqually River in a heavily wooded area. He gave me the map and said, "Good luck."

I headed back to the car with excitement! Finally, we were going to have our camping trip and hopefully I was going to get the answers I was seeking.

## The Campsite from the Dream Emerged

We started our journey down through the entrance of the park and met up with another highway that followed the path of the Nisqually River. As we made the turn, I see that same vehicle from earlier at the gas station is following us once again. I turn to my wife and say, "That vehicle from earlier that I pointed out at the gas station is following us again."

She looks through her rearview mirror and nods to agree.

"That is weird," I said quietly.

At this point in the trip and what's been going on, I don't know if the people had a route like ours or if it was sheer coincidence. I sure did have a newfound understanding that there are no coincidences, just happenings. I take note and proceed. After a short drive, we find the dirt road leading to the sites. We turn off and the vehicle behind us kept going down the road. I concluded at that time that perhaps it was a coincidence after all. We were driving a Ford Mustang with the clearance so low to the ground, that we were feeling every bump and depression. Finally, we make it through without getting stuck. We come up on the campsite along the Nisqually River; it is isolated, deserted, and perfectly located. There is a fire pit and what looks to be a memorial on one of the trees that has the names of two people. I don't recognize the names, so I disregard it and begin the process of starting a fire and erecting the tent. I have my son with me so I put him to work collecting kindling and such for the fire. My wife has been looking over the site and says to me,

"This is exactly what my dream looked like."

I acknowledged what she said and continue working as now it's getting pretty late in the day. We'll talk later as both of us are busy right now. After everything is up and ready for the night, we spend the remainder of the daylight hours attempting to fish in the river and spend quality time with our son and grandson.

# The UFO

It was summer and the sun lingered late in the day. It was around 9:00 PM, as the sun began to set and nightfall was setting in. As dusk came upon us, the colors of the forest, combined with the majestic view of Mount Rainier, which we could see the top of from our site, was just breathtaking and incredible to behold. We put the kids down first and they fell asleep quickly. At around 9:30 PM, my wife and I finally tried to fall asleep. The tent has a sky view and the panoramic span of the stars was as clear as could be. We were far away from any light pollution that we endure in the city. Everything is illuminated to the point our eyes were fixated to the many points of light in the sky. The planes are easy to spot as they move by; the stars, glistening. The planes have the alternating lights on both wing tips that make them indistinguishable from the stars, coupled with their straight-line movement that makes them easy to pick out. As we relax down from our, quite frankly, one of the most exhausting days since I got home from the military, something strange occurs. There it is! As both of are looking to the night sky, a brilliant spherical object came into view. It was white and bright and was much closer than the planes we had previously been seeing before it came into view. The orb was brighter than the moon, yet easy on the eyes. It flew in a zig-zag pattern going in one direction instead of a straight line. It reminded me of a fish attempting to swim upstream, switching back and forth as the currents moved about. It was in both of our view for about ten seconds. I turn to my wife as she is turning to me and ask, "What is that?"

She says, "I don't know." She quite dismissively turns over as it leaves our view and says, "I'm going to sleep now."

I know my wife. She has and holds strict religious beliefs and does not believe in the paranormal. After over fifteen years of marriage, our intimate views have held steadfast and meshed; mine being atheist and hers being Catholic. She did not attend church and I did not preach to her how I thought religions were based on fairy tales. She will tell you she saw something that night, however, will not even begin to speculate what that something is or was. It scared her in a sense and I could see and read that clearly from her face and body language. She needed say nothing else. I got up and told her I wanted to investigate further. I hurriedly put my shoes on and by the time I got outside, the object was gone.

# The Two Voices

Well, now I'm up. I attempted to keep the fire going for another half hour or so; it kept going out. I even poured lighter fluid on the logs that had been burning earlier and that didn't even start the new wood afire. I gave up. I went back inside the tent, removed my shoes, slid into my sleeping bag with my wife and attempted to fall asleep. Slowly I drifted off to sleep. I must have slept really deeply for those few minutes or so, as I am awakened to my wife shaking my arm. She says startled, yet very quietly, "Wake up; there are people behind the tent!"

Now remember we are in an extremely excluded campsite in the middle of nowhere and there was nobody there when we drove in or any signs of anyone being there for a while. By now, I'm half awake. I quickly comply with my wife's intentions of me getting up and looking. It's pitch dark outside and silent. There are no voices or any signs of anyone or anything nearby. There were no flashlights shining from the woods that I could see. The forest was dense and thick with brush. There is no way that anyone could make it around without some kind of light source. I look to her and ask, "Are you sure you heard people?"

Then my son chimes in because he was awakened to the same noises and says, "Dad! I heard them too!"

"What did they sound like?" I ask.

My wife says, "It sounded like two people with southern accents talking."

# The Dream

By this time, everyone is up and spooked. My wife is now insistent that we go to the car and attempt to scare off whoever it is out there by starting the car and turning on the headlights. We head out to the car. She also insists we stay and sleep in the car the rest of the night with the doors definitely locked. It's summertime and near the base of Mount Rainer, the nights are still chilly. I turn on the heater and put the headlights on high beams. Nothing can be seen in the bright lights and I turn them off. I tell them to go to sleep and I'll keep a watch out for anything out the ordinary. I remember staring at the digital clock on the dash as it read eleven PM. I finally nod off after I see everyone from my wife to my grandson and son drift off to sleep.

During this time in my life, it's important to note that I did not dream. To this day, I don't remember my dreams. It's like the process of everything going dark and then seemingly in an instant, waking up. That is what sleep is like for me. I had never had a vivid dream in my life to this point.

As I sleep, suddenly I'm awakened with the most lifelike dream I have ever had. Everything is indistinguishable from reality and I'm looking through my own eyes. I am on all fours in a crouching position. I begin to look up at my surroundings. I see that there is a light above me because everything below me is illuminated. As I look up further, I see a figure in front of me. It is something that resembles a human, yet I can tell that this is not humanlike; nothing I've ever seen, that is. The naked skin of whatever is in front of me is exposed as if it is void of clothing; I see that it has two feet. I see that it is hairless and the color of it is a bluish color. I attempt to move my head upward to see what is in front of me and my eyes gaze upon the anatomy. I see that it has elongated shins, as if the humanlike creature is much taller than me. I am six foot two inches tall and can sense that the creature must be twice as tall as me. As I continue looking upwards toward the shins, I feel restrained and am unable to see the knees of the creature despite me looking upward. Whatever is in front of me seems benevolent. As if I had a second sense about me, I could feel that the being meant no harm. That is how the communication started. I ask, "What are you?"

Instantaneously, my mind is filled with colorful symbols and shapes. I hear it say the words, "King" or "God."

It's fragmented and not precise at this time, because really, this first interaction was communicated to me in a way that was not at all clear at this point. I realized that when it gave the answer to my question, I answered for it in this first iteration of questions. I mouthed the words "King" and then "God" as the shapes and symbols permeated my mind. I realized that it was communicating directly into my mind. It was somehow injecting thoughts into my head and the way in which my mind translated the exchange became the dialogue. I close my mouth for the rest of the exchange and only ask questions to solicit a response. I ask a second question, "Why have you brought me here?"

# Vision One

No sooner had I asked the second question and a flood of shapes and symbols fills my mind's eye and my eyes close within the dream. My mind attempts to read all the information that is being transmitted into my brain, it's too much. I can only manage to see and retain glimpses of the information, as if a movie plays out before me. The creature has given me a vision. I begin to see a great war being fought that encompasses the entire globe. I scan in within my mind and can see part of the vision that is slowed down. I see a building that appears to have been bombed out. The structure's outline shows that it was once a home; now the roof was missing and I could see inside to the contents of the building. There in the kitchen area is a scene, as if frozen in place, yet moving. It is a woman clutching onto two children in the corner. They are trembling and crying out. My vision pans out and I can see the buildings that surround it. Everything in the immediate vicinity is leveled out, as if it had been bombed. Piles of debris and smoke fill the landscape. As I pan out even further, I can see tanks and an army marching towards the building with the woman and two children. The soldiers within the vision are wearing what looks to be gas masks. My vision pans out again, even further this time. This time I see the entire globe of the Earth. I look at the scene and attempt to ingest what I am being shown. The entire globe looks to be set ablaze. I see explosions being set off all over the place and fire lights up the darkness all around.

I open my eyes and I am back in front of the being. I tremble and tears are pouring out of my eyes. I had just been shown what I had perceived as the end of the world and I could feel all the death and destruction. It was rippling through my body. I actually shout out, "Why have you shown me this?"

It pushes me into another instance where shapes and symbols begin to fill my mind. My eyes close briefly and a movie begins to play out within my thoughts. Here I am shown the same fiery sight I was shown in the vision, only this time, I see white lights leaving the Earth. Thousands of these lights are shown and they all fly off the Earth and meet up into a single formation. At the time of this vision, I thought the being was showing me that there was life after death. Since the dream, I have come to other conclusions as seen through my unique filter. I will go into detail about these beliefs towards the end of this story.

# Vision Two

As I begin to open my eyes, my tears subside. I am once again back in front of the being within the base dream. I ask again, "Why have you brought me here?"

Once again I am propelled into my mind and my eyes close. The shapes and symbols are there and a movie within my dream begins to play out. I am looking from afar and I see a black car in a desolate city full of demolished buildings. All the buildings are a tan color and the road is filled with a thick layering of fine dirt. It is a sunny day in the vision and I see myself get out of the black car. Two other men follow me out the car and they are dressed in black suits, wearing sunglasses. My vantage point changes now and I am now looking through my own eyes within the dream. I look down to see what I am wearing and see that I am wearing a white t-shirt, shorts, and a set of sandals. The white t-shirt is torn in spots and appears dirty. I see that I am carrying something in my left hand. It appears to be a tree branch. I later determined that the branch I was carrying was from an olive tree. I look back to the other two that were with me and tell them to stay put. I then proceed to walk down the road that is covered in dirt. I walk a few hundred meters down the path and arrive at a stone wall. As I follow the stone wall, I see a giant green door. I walk up to the door and knock three times with my right hand. The door cracks a little and just as it does, I raise my left hand and announce, "I come in peace. May I enter?"

The door cracks open further and I can see

a man. This man was older, with a well formed beard. He was dressed in religious garb from head to toe, wore a black hat, and had a gown on that was black in color. His dress reminded me of an orthodox Christian priest. He says, "Yes, we have been expecting you."

He gestures for me to enter. He then leads me through a stone courtyard to a building in the center of it. We enter through the doors of the building and then we proceed to a set of stairs located within the building that lead down to the basement of the structure. Once we arrive in the basement, I notice that there is a metallic covering along one of the walls. He walks over the metal covering and opens it and as he does, it exposes the bedrock to the structure. He gestures for me to inspect the bedrock. I look down and notice that what he is gesturing for me to see is a discoloration exposed. The rest of the bedrock is stone in color, or gray. The portion he is pointing towards is black in color. I reach down with my right hand to touch the discolored rock and the entire vision turns into an intense white light. Once again, I find myself back in the base dream in front of the being that had brought me there.

## The Hologram of Jesus

I am confused by now and do not understand what any of that vision meant. I ask, "I don't understand. Who am I?"

This time, the being reaches down with two enormous hands and shows me a device. The device is kind of a reminiscent of an iPad, yet without any buttons or a border on the screen. It reminds me of a piece of glass, only this glass has a picture on it. I look at the picture that is on the screen and can make out that the picture is that of Jesus, at least, what I perceive to be that of Jesus. This is not the historical account of Jesus. The man is darker skinned than the standard narrative of how Jesus is depicted in western culture, yet the features are the same. It is a head shot only and he is wearing a crown of thorns. Confused and perplexed, once again I say with great strength about myself, "I don't understand."

As I look at the picture some more, it changes and the image of Jesus's face morphs into my face, as if I were looking into a mirror. Again I step back, bewildered to say the least, I attempt to understand what I am being shown and what meaning is behind the significance of this exchange. There were no shapes and symbols being transmitted; I am left to my own thoughts. Then and without warning, the entire dream turns into the same bright white light as was experienced at the end of the second vision I was shown and I was awake back inside of my car. I feel a sense of peace overcome my body and mind.

The next moments would be spent remembering what just happened to me in that dream state. I made the trip to find answers and was given many answers during the exchange, yet was left bewildered at what it all meant. Still, I was comfortable with not knowing. As my mind raced through thoughts of attempting to find inner meaning with what had just happened, I noticed something outside of my car as I sat there staring out the window. There it was again. That same spherical white light in the sky that my wife and I had seen the night before was there. It was hovering about one thousand meters above my car and it began to move at quick speed towards the top of Mount Rainier. I watched as the light moved up the mountain, it took about twenty seconds. As soon as it hit the top of the mountain, like a lightning bolt, it shot up in the air and out of sight. I looked at the clock on the car's dash and it read 4 AM.

# The Drive Home

Although I had only had five hours of sleep, I felt refreshed like I had slept for days. I woke my son up and had him help me with packing up the tent and the rest of the camping supplies. Within the hour, we had packed everything up and were back on the road heading towards home. My son, so tired from the whole ordeal, quickly fell back asleep on the drive back.

I then began to tell my wife what had happened the night before in my dream. I could tell through her silence that everything that had happened the previous few days had been hard on her. I could tell her concern, not being able to tell whether or not I was losing my mind, as my actions had changed seemingly overnight.

Spirituality was never my deal; however, the last few days had me rethinking that for sure. I attempted to tell her the dream and she shut me off from talking about it. She told me, "I don't want to hear about it."

Truthfully, all the events were too much to bear. It took me months to attempt to re-engage her over my experience. She is reserved and having been witness to some of the events has left her without an idea as to what really happened on those three days in the summer of 2014.

# Conclusions Made After the Fact

I do not have all the answers to what I experienced that summer. I am left with more questions than answers. I made a Mutual UFO Network sighting report later after the event took place. That report can be found at the following URL:https://mufoncms.com/cgi-bin/report_handler.pl?req=view_long_desc&id=65725&rnd=

You will notice one deviation in the MUFON report and the story I told here. My son came to me a couple of months after the experience and told me that me and him had attempted to start the fire after getting into the car. I have no recollection of that transpiring, so wanted to give only my account on the story. I concluded that his additional narrative would detract from the story as I would be relying on his accounts, which I have no memory of even happening.

This is my first attempt at writing down the entire event as it took place in detail. I have written condensed versions of the story all over the internet. This version is the version that had me reflecting on those days, to the degree where the story can now fully be told.

What I am about to say next might confuse some that are reading this. Depending on your belief system, this may go against that belief. You see, I have concluded that in the first vision, I was shown the "end times." Now, you might be thinking the end times are a fairy tale. The end times are depicted in the three major religions across the globe. I am not a biblical scholar and only read and researched at this time what I felt relevant to my experience. However, the chain reaction of events that transpired after my experience point to other forces at play. I have concluded that whatever I interacted with that night was what would be called an angel or a demon. You see, due to it not being an experience that was viewed as negative, I conclude now that it must have been on the "angel" side of the spectrum. If you ever allow yourself to pick up whatever religious book you may follow after you have an experience like this, you can see through the eyes of a new filter. Are the angels and demons of the Bible extraterrestrials? Wouldn't any being that is not from this place be considered an extraterrestrial?

The many accounts within the Bible, as I will focus on this collection of sixty-six books, paint a very different picture when viewed from this perspective. In that those who influenced these very collected writings could be viewed today as "not of this world". Ezekiel's wheel is a description of a UFO. In Genesis, the word God is translated from the word Elohim, which is the plural form of the word meaning Gods. The Book of Genesis is a knockoff of the Epic of Gilgamesh, which is in turn a knockoff of the Lost book of Enki from the Sumerian cuneiform tablets. Really, what the interaction gave me was a new set of eyes to see the world around me. I am left confused from my interaction, yet quickly see the end approaching us all. You see, the battle for Armageddon is prophesied to occur in what is modern day Syria and what do we see transpiring today? Like I said at the beginning of this experience, I do not have all the answers. I am definitely left with the impression that whatever I experienced was done so for a purpose. Perhaps that purpose is for me to tell the story of what I was shown. Perhaps it was just a dream and a misidentification of a man-made aircraft. My intuition tells me differently and hopefully you have enjoyed me relaying this three day event to you. This is a real account of what transpired during those three summer days in July of 2014. I am relying off my memory for the most part even though the dream has somewhat been seared into my mind like a traumatic event. Writing about that aspect of it is now becoming much more natural and easy to do so. I have changed my belief system since my experience. I now believe in God, only my God and your God may differ in appearance or in definition.

I am convinced we are living in the Biblical

end times. None of what is going on right now makes sense. Who would have ever thought a controversial billionaire would become President? We are primed, and I have been having vivid daydreams lately of a possible scenario I need to share as I think this might become our bleak future.

America is hit with a false flag attack that eclipses 9/11. President Trump is forced to react, but the nature of the false flag has a nuclear implication towards an enemy known to have the fissile material used in the attack. I predict a dirty bomb in a metropolitan area. Trump reacts with one nuclear weapon directed at the source of the nuclear material.

The moment we attack, we will receive incoming nuclear warheads in retaliation from each of our known enemies that have the capability to hit the continental United States. Our retaliatory onslaught of nuclear weapons in response is hindered due to a disconnect and confusion within our military hierarchy.

The electro magnetic pulses that are created with every detonation across the United States will knock out all electronics and electricity, leaving the entire United States in the dark. With America knocked off the world stage and forced to recall all military forces to the homeland, Israel's enemies will attack in force. That is the extent of the reoccurring vision I have been having lately. I will leave you with this:

> "Question everything and never take the official narrative for anything, as things are not *always* as they seem."

This next part of the story involves a dream that I had on the 22 of March, 2015. I was shown a vision and had an out of body experience. The vision was of the entire Earth being hit by a wave of a gold substance. This substance envelopes the entirety of the Earth, and I can then see the religious icons of the Abrahamic religions; a synagogue, a church and a mosque, all being colored in this golden hue. A voice can be heard that says, "See and tell them".

For the next three days, this is what came out of my mind...

# Chapter 1

1. And God said unto them, seek out, and find the one who shall carry forth my will.

2. The messengers of God spread out across all the peoples of all the nations, and watched over the misgivings of man.

3. Men mistreated their brothers, and sold their mothers like cattle are sold in market.

4. Children were gathered together, and slaughtered for the sins of their families, removed.

5. When their leader returned to God, he said "Father, there is no soul among them that is pure".

6. God said, "Son, you must keep searching, for the one who can fulfill the promise which will

become."

7. The leader of heaven then said, "Father, how will I know I have found the one you speak of?"

8. God said, "The moon will fill with blood, the disease and pestilence will increase ten-fold.

9. Still, man will discount this first judgment, and will turn their eyes, so that their spirit will not see the calamity that awaits.

10. Again, I will make the moon fill with blood, and great wars will spread about the land.

11. Still, man will discount this judgment, and will denounce the messengers I sent them before.

12. I will blacken the sun, and all eyes will search out, with amazement, yet none will see the calamity I have unsettled.

13. The anti-Christ will expose himself to the

world, and will lead his people to work against those that I have chosen from the beginnings of time.

14. He is given power over all his tribes, and he will wield a mighty staff, and when he speaks, all will obey.

15. Still, people will live as if nothing has changed for they have lost their faith in me, and for that, I will end this Earth, for all but a select few.

16. Search for this man who will fulfill my promise from those that awaken in the midst of the great deception.

17. For a season, I command you to take your Army, and occupy a tenth of man.

18. Build the great Army over man, and I will protect souls that carry forth the deeds that must pass."

19. The leader of heaven was confused and asked, "What you ask of me takes the fellow messengers down the path for which is entirely against the nature of the righteous."

20. "Their souls are blackened, but surely our control over the multitude will do nothing but hasten their end?"

21. God said, "Son, do not fret over the bodies of the dead, for they had their chance to repent upon the commandments for which I gave them.

22. They made a choice to follow the path to the blackened end when all my messengers spoke of the light being the only path to righteousness.

23. Man does not worship me, because man does not even know I exist.

24. The evil of the souls of those that defy my will, have corrupted the vessel of those who are my

chosen servants.

25. All men will die, who have the souls of the blackness that eats at the side of the enlightened few, will free my chosen of the oppression they have endured.

26. Now, carry forth my will, and all will become evident in due course."

# Chapter 2

1. And the armies of heaven ascended down to watch over the misgivings of man.

2. Unseen amongst the multitude, with the exception of those that were drawn like a moth to a flame.

3. There were many messengers in those days, and the angels of heaven had been working tirelessly to bring about the vision that was bestowed upon them.

4. Some gave the wisdom of the ages to the unrighteous souls as they began to fall for the curse which was placed by God, and was meant to disrupt the spirits of the world from seeing their true selves.

5. God allowed these angels to carry forth their will, as God the creator of the heavens and the Earth, sees everything from inception to conclusion before anything created realizes the existence of themselves.

6. God created the Earth as a refuge for man to walk amongst all the creations of existence.

7. God handed forth the wisdom of the ages of perpetual balances needed for man to realize the perfection of nature.

8. Man had become a breeding ground of generations of division amongst the servants of God.

9. Great wars were fought in the name of their God, and those that wield the power of religion, live like Gods amongst men.

10. They are not the rightful heirs the goodness

bestowed from God's good grace.

11. They have turned their backs upon God's warnings, and worship intermediaries between God and them, and lack the ability to see the error in their ways.

12. The angels began to awaken those that God chose before Adam was firmly put upon land to give lineage to God's will.

13. Some of the corrupt souls began to question what they were shown, and even the angels of his grace, were unable to bring the light to their foreheads.

14. Resistant was man, and prideful, and deceitful, and greedy, and corrupt, and hateful.

15. Still, the angels of heaven tried, and tried, and tried to bring those to the light, for which God had commanded.

16. Those that were awakened were ridiculed, and left to live outside of their blessings, and still man chose to disregard their words as lunacy.

17. When the time comes, in that generation, which is the last generation, all the God's of the Earth, which are not the true God of the lands, will bring forth the sacrifice in their God's name.

18. Still the search continued as the leader of heaven demanded of his servants.

19. Corruption was the food of the day for the distorted masses of his following.

20. Those who donned the armor of God abused those that were left astray.

21. Still, God created each of the judgments so that all would be seen at the same moment by everyone, and there would be much panic amongst the multitude, and people will curse

their God, for they will blame their only connection between them and God as the reason for their woes.

22. Kings of nations stop news from spreading about the judgments of God, this will cause mass confusion amongst the flock, and distrust will envelop all the lands within the Kingdom of God.

23. Hordes of followers will surround and pledge allegiance to the words that are spoken from the anti-Christ.

24. He will talk, and all that are willed to do so, will follow his every-beckoning command, even to take actions against the teachings of their God.

# Chapter 3

1. And then, I saw an angel come out of the hordes of the Army of God's messengers.

2. This angel had eyes of burning fire, and when he spoke to the other angels, they dared not look him in his eyes, for he had the ability to close the doors of heaven within their presence, and he being much greater than they, was given power over any which he encountered.

3. He said unto two angels standing near the river, "Come here, you that stand guard against the resolute righteousness, and tell me if God commanded the angels to carry forth his will, how do you suppose the war will transpire without us following the path to hasten these events?"

4. The two angels immediately, as if being under some spell, set out in search of the souls that will

hasten the judgment from God upon all the men of this Earth.

5. Two leaders will emerge from the flock, both accepted the future that was set in front of them, and between them, they will raise the Armies needed for the final battle on the ground that was already chosen by God.

6. These two men are allowed to punish the sins of man, and the kin of those that sin, so that all will be exposed to the generation as the curse will be lifted, and they will all face the wrath of God's justice.

7. Brother against brother, son against father, all will be full of death, and the rivers will run with the color of the blood from the sacrifice of their Armies.

8. In these times, men will still turn his back on

God, and will deny the messages that were sent from man's beginnings, and will denounce the very existence of God.

9. The angel approached me as I lay witness to his interaction with the other two.

10. I trembled in fear, and bent my knees upon the floor, and dared not look upon his face, for his eyes could find all the flaws within the soul of a man, and had the ability to end a man's existence with only a thought.

11. The angel said, "Come here, son of Adam, and behold what you have missed from what your eyes tell you that you saw."

12. The angels I spoke with, they are my servants, as Angels have kings, just as man has kings.

13. What you saw as death and destruction, or evil doings, were the will of the highest of all the Gods.

14. The people these Angels will stir, are not able to see the light, but were placed here on Earth to bring about God's plan.

15. The souls they take will still have their judgment, but their judgment will begin at the moment of their death.

16. They are a sacrifice unto their God, and are not a sacrifice to the only God, as God recounted his sacrifice, and sent messengers to reveal this to man.

17. They will not be reborn unto another vessel, and if their worldly actions were righteous, then God will reward them, and will give them safe harbor to the new until the number foretold is reached.

18. If their acts are deemed evil, and blackened from their soul to their vessel, God will punish

them by throwing them back into the Earth to await judgment, where they will be the first to be thrown into the sea of fire and will their punishment will be seen by all the people of that day.

19. God is the creator of everything, and anything that can be ever imagined, and the design for man has run its course.

20. Take what you saw here, and tell the people inhabiting the land that was laid out by God, and tell them the warning I have shown.

21. See for yourself that no one will listen, then question what you saw in your vision of me".

## Chapter 4

1. And in those days, God allowed the evil to consume the souls of the dead, and the spirits of those souls, who were blackened by their hate, were allowed to become kings of their lands.

2. God commanded, "Tell the armies to amass, and call out to every tribe, and every nation, and fill the ranks of my Army, so that all will perish upon the Earth.

3. One year, one month, one hour, and one hour from God's commandment, the Army of God's will was allowed to build its ranks, and was allowed to kill innocence in all the lands in order to give warning, liken to a trumpet that all the lands can hear, yet few will listen.

4. And that year, and month, and day, and hour

did not awaken the multitude, as their ears had lost the ability to listen, and their eyes were blinded by the misgivings of the rich, for the rich had gained while their people have suffered, and they have become the God's of worship, and they had led their generations before them astray".

5. Then God commanded, "Release the plague upon the people, and make the plague affect the multitude as punishment for their indiscretions."

6. And the plague set in motion by God, was challenged by man, who had thought that man was the authority, and God did not exist.

7. God saw their actions before they were thought, and changed the direction of the plague, and gave the power to the leader of his army to release the plague against the multitude.

8. Their leader, the great anti-Christ, will be

feared, and worshiped by his people, and will be able to call upon spirits from within the masses of the multitude, and his hate will lead pure souls astray.

9. Wealth will be abolished, as the great wave of deceit will envelop the lands.

10. Souls will be unable to see other souls as being the same, and will begin to hate parts of their soul which is differing then theirs.

11. The fear will grow in the hearts of men, and they will become withdrawn from their physical interactions with their acquaintances.

12. Many, many messengers will be sent, and their message will not be heard.

13. God will have his judgment, and redemption in the field located in the location that man already has knowledge over, and was foretold in

the messages that God sent.

# Chapter 5

1. And the King of heaven stood before God, and asked, "Father, the season is ripe for the promised harvest, in your name, what would you have me do now?"

2. God spoke unto him, "Release the armies, and may they have my blessings, and protections from their adversaries."

3. A great vision was bestowed to the ruler as if a child learns to take their first steps.

4. The great mysteries that only God had completely known.

5. The leader of the armies was ordered to attack those that defied God's existence.

6. The army was given special powers over men,

and when they spoke, all men followed, and were able to kill everyone they saw as unrighteous, unleashing horrors, the likes that have never been seen before by man.

7. The leaders of all the nations, who had allowed the army to grow, were now angry at the actions of God, and had allowed an Army of one hundred nations, the size that had never been amassed before.

8. Porous was their guard, and the soldiers of the army God had commanded were able to kill from deep within their lands at will.

9. Men and women became sickened by the sight of the bloodshed, yet none would demand justice for the slaughtered masses until the tide had already shifted.

10. A man will then be amongst the masses who

will be able to lead God's Army, and will defeat the anti-Christ.

11. God commanded the King of the heavens, "There, that is the man who will bring my judgment to man."

12. The King of the heavens looked down towards the spirit guiding the man on Earth.

13. The man was neither full of sin, nor full of righteousness.

14. Puzzled, he began to measure the man before him.

15. Still, nothing remarkable could be found.

16. The King of the heavens pleaded with God, "What is special with this soul, of this man?"

17. God said unto him, "Look not at what is lacking, but focus on what is there.

18. This man has been born to the generation for which I have condemned, yet his soul is pure.

19. You do not see his soul in this way because he is lacking in greatness, but he has followed the commandments that were given to all of man.

20. I shall turn his greatness on like that of a star racing across the sky, and then all will listen, as he is the witness I have sent to learn of the evil within man, and one that I allowed to be free of the interactions of Angels.

21. He does not know of what awaits his destiny, but his life will bring about greatness that all men will envy, yet their soul will be drawn to his brilliance.

22. He, I have given the knowledge of all, and with this knowledge, he will awaken the masses to their true nature.

23. He will free the armies of their will to fight with one breath, and he will extinguish the punishment I have commanded over man, but not until judgment is waged, and the debt owed is paid."

# Chapter 6

1. The Lord of the angels came down to the Earth to welcome this soul into this world, and assigned seven angels to watch over his soul as he was born unto man, yet his birth was hastened due to the darkness that the watchers had placed in his wake.

2. God had given this soul freedom from all the manipulation from the heavens and had allowed the darkness to surround the soul of this man, and the angels of heaven could do nothing but watch, and watch they did.

3. God set forth the temptations of this soul, and gave this soul freedom from the manipulation of the other men of the Earth, yet he was without the religions of this Earth, and their influence, as they

had become distractions to the masses that inhabited all the land, and he saw the corruption, and lies, and deceit in other men.

4. In those days, religions of the Earth had become a thorn in the side of God, and the men who were given the messages to carry forth, had been deceived, and the messages had been manipulated, and the men of the Earth had been led astray, having believed the words of men despite the truth of the messages that had been sent, they chose to follow the words of man, and they mock the words of God.

5. And, this man who was without guardian from heaven, did live amongst the men of the evilness inhabiting this Earth, and he found no refuge from their wickedness.

6. The darkness was permitted to carry forth

temptations to test this man, and other men who followed the darkness were permitted to carry forth the deeds which God did permit.

7. God told the angels who were tasked to watch, helplessly as temptation was presented by the darkness that had consumed the souls of the men of the Earth.

8. The seven Angels of heaven were allowed to give the righteous choice as if a thought to the man, but were not allowed to interact, or intervene.

9. Once, every seven years, this man was given a choice, and this choice was met with each of the sins which God had given warning over within his books.

10. This man would be tested, and there was no God for which to turn to, for he had denied the

existence of a God that would allow the suffering to cover the land, and the wickedness to inhabit the evil souls of man.

11. For every period of seven, one angel of heaven would be given the power to intervene once the moment had presented itself.

12. They would be allowed to visit this man, within his dreams, but were not permitted to reveal the destiny of this man, and were not allowed to tell of the wonders of heaven, they were only allowed to show the man the righteous path, and it was up to his soul to make the choice, and the choice would be measured against the commandments of the God of all, and judgment would be passed upon the evil souls of the Earth, but punishment would be held at bay until the final battle foretold.

13. Five judgments were imposed upon this man, each consisting of seven years, and each time, this soul remained righteous, and for this, his path was full of pain, and his life was full of loneliness, and of awkwardness, and he did fit like a square peg within the sphere of the entirety of the Earth.

14. Man was permitted to lead him astray, and none of the Angels of heaven were permitted to interact, for God had laid out his will and they did obey.

15. On the fifth period of seven, the gates to heaven were opened, and the last two angels who had not acted on the previous judgments passed down from God, were allowed to send forth a message to this man, but only if this man asked the questions.

16. The angels waited for the moment when the

man, who had lived without the light of God, and without the guidance from the angels of heaven, to ask the questions that would allow their message to be received.

17. The man, who had been without God's favor, and had been led astray by the misgivings of other men, had never asked for God, for he had been led down a path without the light, and became knowledgeable over the nature of other men.

18. The angels commanded those who interacted with the man, to carry forth their will, and to take all the good fortune the man had, leaving him with nothing but despair.

19. On the sixth month, after God had released the angels to interact with this man, when all had looked the other way, as calamity, after calamity had been allowed to build within the soul of the

man, this man did call out, "God, why have you forsaken me"?

20. And, God himself did reach down to the son of man, and did wipe away the tears from his face, and said, "Son, I have awaited this day since I created you in my image.

21. I have made you lose everything so that I could show you the evil that resides in man, for without this knowledge, you would be unable to fulfill the role for which you will play to carry forth my will.

22. I have sent two angels, and they will guide you down the path for which you must take."

# Chapter 7

1. A man had come from the masses of the elite, and had come from little wealth to lead a nation of great might.

2. Like a bear, this man had the tongue of silver, and his people did love his stature.

3. His grip was strong enough to break the hand of the other leaders of the World, and his stare was able to invoke fear deep within their souls, but his words were inspiring, and his people did love him so.

4. He, God had given the knowledge of all the Earth, and to him, he gave the power of the sun, to bestow his wrath as he saw fit, but ultimately he was restricted to act upon the beckoning of God's will.

5. And, so he waited for the signs of the stars, and was given unlimited knowledge from which he could steer his massive Army, and he built his Army out of the masses who did adore his strength.

6. Within his land, he invoked the strength of unity, and began to build upon his resolve.

7. The leaders of the Earth were driven to keep him from his destiny he would think at night, yet he was conflicted from which way to react to these messages as they were given.

8. A messenger was sent to bestow upon him the secrets of his enemies, and he did take in the message of deceit for which he learned, and he did see the manipulation the evil leaders of the Earth did play.

9. He had the power of the sun, and could drop

the destruction from the sun upon man at his beckoning, and men did fear this, and submitted under his threat.

10. The other nations of the World, did take from the wealth of the nation, and this leader sought to punish their efforts.

11. Knowing that they were afraid of his power over the sun, they allowed him to take over nations, and to expand his empire.

12. Like a thief in the night, his nation did take over lands that were promised, and he did increase his flock, and his people rejoiced as unity set upon the land.

13. God, had already foreseen all of this and his Army was allowed to grow, and increase in strength, and great power was given over his Armies, and all the world's armies trembled in

fear, for they knew what had to be done, but were reluctant in standing against the powerful leader and his Army.

# Chapter 8

1. And God did show the son of man, all the workings, and the secrets of all things, and his spirit grew, and he became humbled.

2. For now he could see the troubles of his woes were only there for they bore the will of God, and all things have light, and have dark, but they are all a part of the plan, for which was set forth for us to follow.

3. The balance was the will of God, and man had become corrupt in the pursuit of all control over the masses, and deceit laid out in front of the weak spirits can lead to control, which leads to the oppression of the all the men of Earth.

4. All men were created in the image of Adam, and Adam is the kin to all.

5. Somehow man had come to think that they were alone in the universe, and that they were not unique within the multitude of animals, and plants, and even the very ground they stand upon, does not beckon their spirit to look towards the truths that are plainly visible to the watchful eye.

6. For three days, he did walk with God, in heaven, and his spirit did ask many questions, as all was shown to him.

7. Stripped of his indiscretions, he was left with the guidance, and knowledge of the God of all Gods, and the true creator of everything, and anything.

8. God told this man that there would be signs which would show him the route that he should take, and when the light shows the way, follow the light.

9. Three periods of three await him, along his journey, he will be given the wisdom of the heavens.

10. The first, will open the doors to learning of nature, and of the corruption within the hearts of man.

11. The second, will allow him to expose this corruption and deceit, breaking the spell that had been cast over all the people of all the lands.

12. And the third, will lead down the path to reclaim the throne that was taken from the creation of God, and to kill the anti-Christ which had been given an Army to kill a third of the men of the Earth.

13. The man left the encounter with God, and did question the events he was shown, and he did question his sanity, as his experience did conflict

with everything he had come to know.

14. A war consumed his soul, as one part of the man knew the truth, and accepted the task he was given, while the other was reluctant to accept a seemingly unachievable task, as he knew the nature of men to discount anything they did not experience themselves.

15. Still, God's plan would lead this man to the destiny foretold, and his path would be laid out for he had been taken out of the control of other men, and his power to speak was limited to those who had ears to hear.

# Chapter 9

1. And all these things were shown to the son of man, and his thirst grew for knowledge over the god's of men, and the knowledge of these teachings called upon his beckoning.

2. He gained knowledge over the ways in which the will of God is transcended upon the dwellers of the Earth, and how God had influenced all the actions of the men before him.

4. He saw the watchers of men, who God had commanded to carry forth his will, and he saw that some within the flock had seen these messengers too, but their eyes were not able to see them for what they are, they only questioned the deceit they held within their hearts.

5. He measured the men of the dwellers of the

Earth, and saw their indiscretions as with a new set of eyes, one that had been purified by the grace of God, almighty.

6. In the shadows he dwelt, and conflicted he was, as the path that laid before him seemed impassable, and truly there was no way from which he could place himself into power over others, so he remained silent and awaited the signs from heaven to unfold, and the guidance of the angels to show the path to the promise of God.

7. He saw the two angels that were ordered by the King of Heaven to occupy the two souls who would bring about the battle that brings out the judgment of man.

8. These two men represent the leaders of great nations that have no borders, for their grasp goes beyond borders of man, and their reach talks

directly to the soul of those that have ears to listen.

9. The first, was the angel who was leading the soul of the anti-Christ, and his Army was allowed to build for a time.

10. The sun became dark, and the first period of heaven was given to this man, and his words were allowed to become written.

11. The awakening of the spirit of the men who have ears to hear will open their eyes as a child born into the world, and with their new eyes, they will see all that has been hidden.

12. A great shock will overcome those that read the words of his conjecture, as power was given unto him to lead the Chosen who would become the keepers of the living, and would carry forth the will of God, free of the judgment that awaits

all the sinners of the Earth.

13. And he said, "Hear what I say, for today is the day of your atonement.

14. Sons and daughters of man, you have been warned from times past to follow your heart, and to live within the voice of reason.

15. You have been shown the power of the God of everything, and have chosen to follow the deception that was placed before you.

16. How selfish of a man, whose roots are that of Adam, to deceive another of the same flesh, desiring personal riches, when all the riches mean nothing to the souls of heaven, thou has been deemed wicked before God.

17. I ask you now, to repent upon the sins that you have committed, and thou shalt be saved from the calamity that awaits.

18. Time is short, as the heavens have already begun to bring forth the hour of the God above heaven, and death and destruction will envelop the Earth, and all the Earth's armies, and all the people of the Earth will be destroyed."

19. Hear my plea, repent in your ways, and release your hate, for the hour is here, and man will be judged without mercy."

# Chapter 10

1. And, the man who God had plucked from the multitude to gather and awaken the servants of God to the hour of the great judgment, was unable to draw the ears who were put hear to listen, and he became increasingly frustrated.

2. This is the great confusion that God spoke of to the Angels of heaven that had closed the eyes of the Earth's inhabitants, and allowed the darkness to set.

3. Man had become Godlike in their conviction, and have received the distorted message from their leaders, and have given up on the truth of God and the mysteries.

4. None were allowed to see the words, but were able to see if only their eyes would follow the soul that guides them.

5. The son of Adam, looked up to God, with defeat in his eyes, and said, "God, why has your message been met with such distrust?

6. Have the creations that you made become so vain that they cannot see that their creator is bringing forth the hour of their judgment?"

7. God said, "Son of Adam, I see that you have taken what I showed you, and been met with the deafness of the multitude.

8. The troubles you see, and the blindness that falls on those that hear your words spoken, is by design.

9. Have faith in the plan that I have set before you, and read the holy scriptures of their beliefs, for they have been led astray, and only the ears who are drawn to the message will receive the message.

10. The darkness keeps the majority of the multitude from seeing what is plainly in sight, and that is due to the way in which man was designed.

11. I shall give you this gift, and this gift will take forth your message, and will give credence to your warning amongst the dwellers of the Earth.

12. I have set in motion, a series of four signs, and one sign in between.

13. These signs will bring forth the warnings of the three religions that dominate the face of the Earth, but are not true to me, and they worship the writings of men, and the words of men, because they fear my judgment upon their souls.

14. The first, I will turn the moon to blood, and with this coming of the sign from heaven, I will release the plague unto a part of man, and this plague will be allowed to grow, and man will run

from those that it inflicts, and will act as if

nothing has happened.

15. The second, I will turn the moon to blood, and

with this coming, the armies of their end will be

allowed to build, and two angels will be released

to guide my servants and bring forth my

judgments across the land.

16. Still, no man will see the judgments that are

presenting themselves, and people will hear of

rumors of wars, and will deny what is happening

is connected to their God, who they worship so.

17. To split up the signs for which I have

presented, I will darkens the Sun upon the face of

the land that will be first to feel the judgment of

my will.

18. People will look upon the signs I have given,

and will still deny my wrath, and I will hear

deception in their voices as they cry out to me, and I will hear their pleads for good fortune, and selfish wants, and they will give nothing to my merit, and I will allow the third moon to fill with blood.

19. With the coming of this third moon, I will unleash the punishment upon those that I gave the warning to, and their money will have no value, and the merchants will sell no goods, and people will turn to the darkness inside of them.

20. Wars will engulf a third of the lands of all man, and still no one will accept the judgment that is on the horizon, and they will still deny me.

21. The forth warning will go out across the land, as I will fill the final moon with the blood of my final warning to the inhabitants of Earth.

22. The prophesied leader will emerge, and will

stand up in his conviction, and will lead the Army to the north, and they will consume the lands to their east, and with that, the king to the south, who was also prophesied, will stand, building his Army awaiting the final battle that will invoke my judgement."

# Chapter 11

1. The ancient one is awakened with the shaking of the earth.

2. Smoke, ash, brimstone rain upon the plains, and those that inhabit the Earth become troubled.

3. The great Army fills the masses, turning brother upon brother, and son upon father.

4. A great division fills the air.

5. The war is soon, they say.

6. The war is false, they exclaim.

7. The war is old, they complain.

8. The Army builds, and spreads as a virus plagues mankind.

9. Many will die, and more will cry to the heavens,

but none to God.

10. They will curse each other, and will hate all they do not understand.

11. Their anger will be met with anger, and their hate will be met with hate.

12. One third of the lands will be consumed with war, yet they will deny, and will think only of self.

13. A man arises out of the horde of the untrusting, and the discarded.

14. This man will lead the Army that plagues mankind to great victories as the plague is allowed to spread the hate, and death.

15. Will no man, or no Army stand against them, they will yell.

16. Like a swarm of locusts, the Army will consume a third of the lands.

17. Lightning fast they are, and without fear of death they have become, and no man will be able to speak reason into their minds, for they are the Army of judgment upon the wickedness of the men before them.

# Chapter 12

1. Let it be known.

2. The man that seeks power over other men with pride, shall be shackled to that pride as those around them become greater.

3. The man that seeks selfless redemption, shall inherit gifts of foresight, and shall become victorious over deceit.

4. The man that seeks wealth, shall inherit the title of hated, and despised.

5. The man who steals from those who enter his home, will be without a home.

6. Those that follow the light, will be awakened by the light, and the light will give them grace and solitude.

7. The man who lusts, shall inherit the plague of lust, and will lust after the power and the money of the other two.

8. The man who draws no faith from self, will be of the Earth and nothing more.

9. Only those that give up their earthly self, will be allowed to enter the Kingdom above.

10. Only those who discard all earthly pleasures, all wants, and all desires, will inherit the lasting life.

11. True love is the key to paradise, as love is the most powerful force of all creation.

12. True love for your enemies, releases your vile of wickedness.

13. True love for the lands and all that lives within releases the vile of pride.

14. True love for all of creation and all you are faced with releases your vile of the darkness.

15. Only those who are designed in that way, will be able to follow as instructed.

# Chapter 13

1. And, the king said, "Let the heavens rain down upon a third of man".

2. A great mountain was thrown from the heavens into the sea, and a great earthquake was felt by everyone.

3. Everyone stopped, and stared at the sky, as a great vision was shown, and within this vision all were shown the true coming.

4. Men trembled, and ran to the mountains to hide from the coming.

5. The seas were strewn upon the lands of great empire, destroying with impunity.

6. The great empire will be crushed in a second, and punishment for the sins of them that dwell,

and those that dwelled before them will be swift as God is merciful.

7. Those that are found worthy, will enter the heavens above, and enter into the kingdom of God.

8. The entire world will watch as she is killed, and no one will do anything but watch in awe.

9. This will happen at his beckon, when the battle is all but lost.

10. The King will descend upon the men that dwell, and he will impose his judgment upon those that live through that hour.

11. Those who find the light will be drawn to their path to safety from all that will happen in an instant.

12. The collapse of all mankind will be swift, and

the all life that lives upon the Earth.

13. All those souls will be judged upon their works, and those found worthy will be allowed to oversee the new beginning of the Earth.

14. The light bearers will be risen to heaven to receive their promise, and will inherit all that they know to be true.

15. They will inherit the powers of the heavens and will start a new kingdom in the new beginning.

16. Saved from the calamity, and eternally blessed, those that seek, will become troubled, and those that become troubled, will become amazed, and those that gain the knowledge to the tree of life will surely inherit eternal life in the kingdom of God.

# Origins

Understanding the beginnings of this experience (life) seems to be a function of organisms that have become self-aware. Somewhere through the life processes, and the processes seen from the observation of the conscious mind, a desire to seek an understanding of why the individual identity has been allowed to exist, will cross the thought processes of whoever searches far enough for the answers.

An infinite amount of ways in which to view this existence are available and at your disposal. Yet, our minds are geared towards associating what is generally taken as the "mainstream" answer that conforms to our own social identity. This social identity is heavily influenced by locally-derived cultural norms that are mimicked within smaller groupings of identity. Even our subjective viewpoints of reality, differ from person to person. Subtle differences occur between two individuals that may or may not conform to a shared identity along the chain of compartmentalized identities that are all possibilities. The mind compartmentalizes all aspects in this reality--to keep you in a linear order of existence.

Consciousness is something that is enjoyed by self-aware life. Our reality consists of a series of biological processes that work in unison to allow for the creation of our conscious minds. It is foolish for us to see our personal lives as unique when everything that we can see in the physical world works for, and is a part of larger orders of identity.

For instance, all the cells that make up the human

body are not alike. They are all bound to work together within the body system dictated by your genetic DNA coding. The cells within your lungs have a set purpose, and live within a concealed environment. Individual cells work together for the organism, which in this case is that of the identity of being a lung.

Who is to say that those same lung cells are not conscious beings who utilize their senses to perform the function dictated by the higher order to their existence? We feed a higher order of existence much like that of the analogy given above. We feed a series of consciousnesses that culminate with the consciousness of the entirety, as we are a remnant of the energy that has been here since the very beginning.

When we die, we assume our role within the higher order of consciousness. Consciousness is compartmentalized along lines of identity. Anywhere that multiple consciousness minds collude, enables the creation of a new consciousness to take shape. That is a life form as it absorbs energy, and gives off energy by all its moving                    parts. If you were to think about the concepts I am talking about here; and open your eyes to the truth, you would see that *We are a part of the consciousness that runs the entirety of existence. We all live on within that paradigm.*

The first order of identity you have as you look outside of self is that of your family. This, of course, is in the beginning. Minds work together to set order and routine into the mix. Norms are realized and the unit begins to think alike. All in appearance between acceptable and unacceptable behavior. The energy given freely by the minds of the members works as the life force for the organism. This life force is fluid. It cannot be seen with the naked eye just as WiFi cannot be seen, but does exist.

Scale up that view, and you will begin to see another life force emerge with social groupings of identity. Then nationalism, race, heritage, etc..., then after a long road of discovery, and finally after all those identities have been realized, you will eventually find the highest order for your kind in realizing you are a part of the human species.

Take it further up along the chain of consciousness, and we become an animal of the Earth, then become life on Earth, then eventually, the Earth itself. If you keep scaling upwards through all the known processes that exist above the order of humans, and you will see that that consciousness starts to get exponentially larger as you scale out.

If you keep searching for roots of identity and how you are a part to that higher order, as without you, the organism would not be complete, and without it, you would not exist. There is a mutually beneficial relationship between you and all of consciousness in that way. You will eventually see that the entire universe constitutes one consciousness, and you and the rest of humanity are a part of that conscious mind.

You and I live on. We all live on as we feed a higher order of existence. One that does not live and die a short seventy years, but has been here since the beginnings, and will be here long after your physical form is gone...

We see such a narrow view of existence in general. Our senses do not allow us to experience the entirety to the complexity that surrounds us. The fundamentally shared commonality between all living, conscious beings, is the energy that is shared. Energy is information, which is data, which is mechanically driven.

We are the result of processes of a mechanical nature where multiple groupings of cellular life are working in synchronicity to achieve a common goal. These processes have allowed for the formation of the self-identity. Self-identity is not unique to humans and is found in all examples of self-programming lifeforms.

Consciousness is not unique to humans, and it is easy to see the cyclic nature of this existence. An endless paradigm of interlocking cycles makes up our 3D reality. We live in a reality dictated by cause and effect. Everything is the result of a cause. Consciousness must exist on higher orders of existence because it exists at our level. That is the proof.

As above, so below.

Take the newfound understanding that we are components to higher orders of consciousness based on the model seen within the orchestration of dependent processes carried out by various living organisms within the human body, as well as the concept of "cause and effect" being the driving force for realization, then you can finally arrive at the position necessary to view the series of conscious organisms for which you belong.

Self-identity is the first stop in the series of identifications possible along the chain of identity for which we all feed. We can choose to view our existence from this stance, and for the most part, people do live within this protective bubble of existence for entire lifetimes. We create spheres within this existence. These spheres represent our social influences, and for the most part, we are in control over the direction these spheres take, or so it would seem.

The mind gives the individual identity the illusion of control. Since we do exist within the paradigm of causation resulting in realization, and knowing that humans are programmable creatures, further uncovers a system where the organism uses individual identities to further itself, and its understandings at the higher order of identity. A picture starts to emerge whereas it becomes easy to identify with the next higher order of consciousness which does not reside at the scale of human kind, but is compartmentalized and is not shared among most of the populace.

Division exists from the perspective of the human

organism. The compartmentalized mind that took shape and propelled early humans to create is dividing the populace up into factions of resistance, all working independently to direct the forward momentum for the organism.

Ideas are like viruses and antibodies that the organism creates and introduces through an orchestrated result achieved through multiple processes working in tandem. Individual identity keeps the organism fluid, and keeps the linear movement of the organism appearing to be moving in a progressive manner, but really that is an illusory observation given that change is inevitable and it is us who determines what is advancement and what is regression.

Once you identify the organism for which you are a component for, you can view the moving parts that make up the consciousness for that collection of bodies. Every living body is a component to higher orders of consciousness. Identifying who manipulates the direction the organism takes by utilizing the "cause and effect" modeling makes the identification of the "heads" for these organisms clearer at lower levels of existence, but remains increasingly harder to identify at higher orders of identity. In this case, "higher orders" references both size and scope.

This relationship is easily seen in political movements across the spectrum of societal structures. We divide naturally into social orders of identification. Magnetic attraction seems to be present as we find our place within our social order by a series of sequential events that seem to be unique to everyone. Alignment leads to higher orders of identification taking shape which feeds the newly identified collective consciousness.

People become the moving parts making up the body of the life force, and their movements within their own hierarchical division within the structure, advances the movements across the higher orders of identification.

"Left, right, center" are all terms for which we use to align with on one order of conscious identity that exists along the spectrum. This divisive list represents the two poles that exist within each of us. The negative and the positive energies. The up, down effect that is experienced within our emotional makeup. This is the larger order to the modeling seen within each of us. A person can look at their self to identify the universal modeling for everything that exists around us. We even compartmentalize this knowledge into professional fields which is why you rarely see a biologist who is also an astronomer. Those that start making the connections for the blueprints found across all fields of study are typically ostracized out of the order of identity within their fields.

These defense mechanisms found within these higher orders of consciousness all carry out a function to keep the organism in a linear order of existence. Advancement is the outcome and within closely-knit scientific circles, anything outside of the accepted norm, will be attacked by the rest of the organism in an order to keep the organism from moving in an "unapproved" direction. Everything is relatable and dependent upon other processes in this existence, as this existence is dictated movements and collisions resulting in a realization.

Consciousness drives reality. Everything that we can create on this Earth has its origins within the thought construct. It takes consciousness to create a thought as far as we can determine, and this relationship is easy to visualize given that everything that is man-made, was thought out before it was created. We reshape matter to configure it in a manner to add value which is determined by the physical cost associated with its creation mixed with perceived worth which we c o l l e c t i v e l y  a g r e e  u p o n. If it takes consciousness to create something out of seemingly nothing, then what does that say about the creation seen within the universe? If the template we must work from shows us that we create, and our creation originates in a thought, which is virtual space, then is it hard to see that this relationship between thought and creation exists in all examples of manifestation? In the beginning, there was thought and this thought created everything in existence. Thought drives creation.

What is consciousness? To my understanding, consciousness is derived in the operating center of the body which is the brain. Bio-chemical reactions take place producing an electromagnetic field. I believe that the consciousness that runs your body exists within this field. This field cannot be seen with the naked eye, but does exist. Electromagnetic energy is quantifiable in my opinion, and represents streamed data.

Our existence is a collection of information or data for which we derive our understanding of this reality. Our bodies use sophisticated processes of lower life forms which work in unison to enable the bodily construct. Electromagnetic energy is produced through biochemical processes produced by the bodily system. This "virtual" space is where thoughts originate. Thoughts that shape the world around you.

We are all coded along this path we call life. We ingest information for the world that surrounds us on a constant basis. We adapt to our surroundings and the person you identify with today, will change as time passes. This is inevitable. The present concept is always fleeting from the perspective of the self. Even our conscious thoughts are playing catch up to the true operating system of that of the subconscious mind. The subconscious runs the show, and the conscious mind gives us the illusion of control.

We enter this world with the genetic traits that are carried down from both parents. This becomes the blueprint for your operating system. You then start the process of experiencing life, whereas all information is gathered from your personalized interactions with the world around you. This experience gained is information stored into your memory which is later utilized as a basis for which to formulate answers for choices going forward. Negative interactions are foremost accessible within the conscious construct within the memory field. This field of information, or field of memory produced by biological processes is utilized by the subconscious construct on a constant basis to formulate answers and to facilitate movement of the body. We latch onto negativity as a defense mechanism attempting to stop past experiences from repeating in a cyclic manner.

We all have our own personalized versions for what is real, which we have invested energy into. Our own understanding and rationalization to why we exist in the first place are examples of this. Once that acceptance, whatever that is, takes shape, will not unseat easily from the subconscious mind. We are programmable creatures, and are heavily influenced by environmental factors that dictates our behavior. The cause/effect relationship holds true as well, and emotions drive our reactions. Emotions are heavily dictated by our identity of self. The left/right brain duality along with how neuroplasticity affects your ability to take on additional information once the neuro pathways become well-formed and rigid, are how the mind works against itself when presented with contradictory information that goes against the held narrative. So, there are physical constraints involved once you have set the parameters for what is real, and what fails to fit your own personal paradigm.

The current self for which you identify with, can be quantified as the information you have accumulated over the span of your entire life added with the genetic modeling you received at conception. Our minds are the operating systems for which are limited by the amount of knowledge gained over the course of our lives. People are predictable in the larger context. The mystery resides in the quantification of this information. How would one give a numerical value to an interaction? These are the great mysteries that we are not privy to understanding given that our current understandings do not facilitate a study into the quantification of action. Theoretically, one could predict the course of action for a single person if their entire memory and genetic predispositions were quantified, and scenarios themselves were quantifiable. It boggles the mind to think that we are given the illusion of control, but our programming gained from both genetic factors mixed with experiential data drives our movements through this existence.

A beautiful orchestration of biological processes allows for the creation of a shared consciousness, ultimately identifying as a single being. Identity dictates alignment with viewpoints on reality having an overarching impact on the direction taken by the host organism. Interpretation of the physical environment coupled with genetic traits gives the impression of a personalized experience. This is a byproduct of the mechanism, and is essential for an organism, no matter what level of identity, to grow. Competing energies colliding produces new energies. Energy is our basic form. One commonality all matter has is energy. This begs the question, "What are we?"

To describe the "what" when answering the question "What are we?" we must realize that whatever definition we derive, is always dependent upon the observational point we take as the observer. A rock studied with the naked-eye will derive a different definition than one studied under a microscope. That is the nature of observational energies. Energy surrounds our existence, and it is that energy that we observe which we derive conclusions to make sense of it all.

One could say, "We are energy in our basic form" and be just as right as someone who garners the more classical definition of us being a biological being. Conformity within the organism created through identity and competing factions within the organism's structure leads individuals within that grouping of identity to accept the agreed

153

upon narrative and definition to support their version of what is right and what is wrong.

There are infinite ways in which to observe our surroundings, but we are limited to what our internal programming allows. If I were to say, "We are biological machines" this might garner a reaction that immediately disputes and defeats the notion within your conscious mind; if it goes against your held beliefs. But, if you take it from the prospective that the body is a series of biological processes carried out by differing systems working to achieve a common goal of enabling your shape to take form, then you can begin to see that the observation of us being machines makes a little more sense. It is not the right answer, but is an observational point for which a description was derived. There are no right answers, just competing observations.

So, wherever these formations of complex energy-beings manifest along the many overlapping orders of identity, we can gain a newly-found perspective into the processes that allow the newly discovered "organism" to exist. By taking the perspective that observational points dictate interpretation, one can determine what functioning exists to allow the higher-order to exist and thrive through its lifecycle. Make no mistake that these energy-organisms do interact within this physical world, as discussed earlier, all creation has origins in the virtual space of thought-energy.

Everything is cyclic. It is here in a moment, for a time, then gone in relation to the universe itself. Cycles create patterns for which our minds are geared to identify. We are limited in our field of studies as we have neglected the study of the cyclic nature of the universe, and that relationship to the intelligence that exists within the inner-working inherent in that narrative. Something had to give this reality its physical laws. We are limited to the observation of these laws, but that is where the narrow visioning of what that looks like ends.

To say, "A series of laws working in tandem created everything you see in this reality" without questioning why the laws are the way in which they are, is like saying "We can see these laws that seem to behave in a way that is without intelligence, because we say so." Disregarding the relationship seen with mankind's own creations whereas thoughts drive creation. I know the concept of what holds a consciousness is debatable, but I contend that everything that is alive and made of matter which creates an electromagnetic field, is conscious. Even dead bodies within this matrix add to the collective pie of existence and have a rebounding effect upon the larger identity within the organismic system. If you had to visualize what this concept would look like, it would be best represented by a series of spheres overlapping into infinity, as the universe is currently in a state of growth, or expansion. It too has a lifecycle. Everything that exists follows these principles.

The end of humanity as we know it is upon us. I am the author of this very important book... https://www.amazon.com/dp/B07L7W88W1

Made in the USA
Middletown, DE
31 July 2021